Chores Around the House

Alyson King

Rourke
Publishing LLC
Vero Beach, Florida 32964

www.rourkepublishing.com

PHOTO CREDITS: © Hortongroup: page 2; © Armentrout: page 3, 5, 7, 9, 13, 17, 19, 21; © Lisa F Young: page 15, 17; © Charity Myers: page 23

Editor: Robert Stengard-Olliges

Cover design by Nicola Stratford

Library of Congress Cataloging-in-Publication Data

King, Alyson L.
 Chores around the house : the world around me / Alyson L. King.
     p. cm. -- (The world around me)
 ISBN 1-59515-992-4 (Hardcover)
 ISBN 1-59515-963-0 (Paperback)
 1. Table setting and decoration--Juvenile literature. 2.
Orderliness--Juvenile literature. 3. Helping behavior in children--Juvenile
literature. I. Title.
 TX871.K56 2007
 642'.7--dc22
                                    2006022156

Printed in the USA

CG/CG

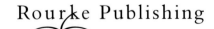

Rourke Publishing

www.rourkepublishing.com – sales@rourkepublishing.com
Post Office Box 3328, Vero Beach, FL 32964

Table of Contents

Introduction

In families, everyone has **chores** to do. Kids can do lots of chores to help out around the house like setting the table, clearing the table and cleaning your room. When everyone helps on the chores, more time is spent having fun!

Setting the Table
with Charlie

Charlie knows it is time for his dinnertime chore when his mother puts plates and glasses on the kitchen counter. They remind him it is his job to set the table!

Charlie's mother puts the plates and glasses out where Charlie can reach them. He can get everything else himself. Charlie goes to the kitchen drawer and counts out four forks, four spoons, and four dinner knives. He carries all twelve **utensils** to the table.

Next, Charlie puts two plates and one **napkin** at each family member's spot. He folds the napkins in half. The napkins go on the right side of each plate. Charlie is ready to put the utensils out now. The fork is on the left side of the plate, the knife and spoon sit on top of the napkin.

9

Charlie checks the table to make sure he has remembered everything. Oops! He forgot to put out the glasses. Charlie puts a glass at the top of each plate above the knife and spoon. Now Charlie's dinnertime chore is **complete**.

Clearing the Table with Acacia

Acacia knows it is time for her dinnertime chore when everyone has finished eating dinner. Now it is time for Acacia to clear her dishes from the table. Acacia puts her plate on the counter next to the sink.

13

Washing the Car with Sarah

Sarah knows its time for her weekend chore when her mother brings out a bucket of soapy water and a brush. That reminds her that it is her job to wash the car.

After washing the car with soapy water Sarah rinses the soap off with clean water. Then she drys the car with a towel. Now the whole family is proud of their car.

Tidying Up my Bedroom with Juan

Juan knows it is time for his end of the day chore when his dad reminds him it's almost bedtime. Juan looks around his bedroom to see what needs to be put away.

First Juan puts all his toys back in their box. He puts the box in the closet with his shoes and closes the door. Then he stacks the books neatly on his bookshelf and puts all his small toys in his nightstand.

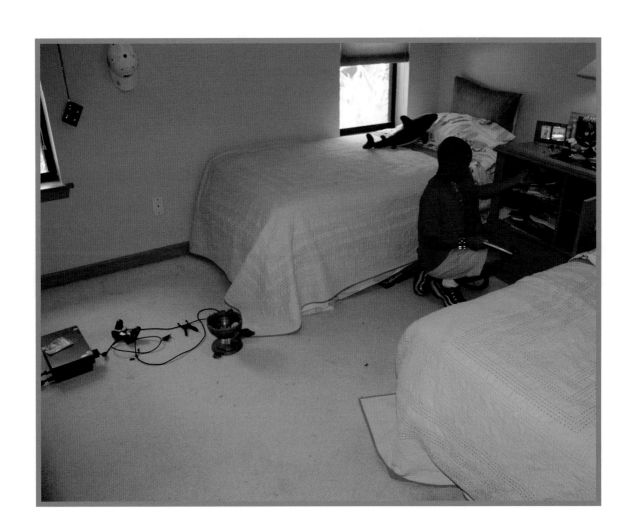

When our chores are all done our family plays together outside.

Every family has chores to do. What chores do you choose to help out with at your house?

23

Glossary

chore (CHOR) —a job that has to be done regularly
complete (kuhm PLEET) —finished or done
napkin (NAP kin) —a paper cloth used to wipe hands and lips
 while eating
utensils (yoo TEN suhl) —tools used to eat or cook

Index

Further Reading

Mayer, Mercer. *Helping Mom*. McGraw-Hill, 2002.
Spafford, Suzy. *Helping-Out Day? Hooray!* Scholastic, 2003.

Websites To Visit

http://www.familyfirst.net/parenting/chorelist.asp
http://www.youthonline.ca/parents/chores/index.shtml

About The Author

Alyson L. King has taught and counseled students in a variety of settings, from Kindergarten on the Penobscot Reservation in Maine to middle grade students in the Florida Keys. Alyson is a fulltime mother to three beautiful girls and, along with her husband, has parented over twenty wonderful children through the foster care system.